THE ECHOES OF THE MIND

THE ECHOES OF THE MIND

SHINY BHATTACHARYA

1

*T*he Echoes of the Mind
    True Being Beyond the Veil of Thought
By Shiny

2

Copyright © 2025 by Shiny

All rights reserved. No part of this book may be reproduced in any form or by any means without permission from the author, except for brief quotations used in reviews or articles.

First Edition – 2025

ISBN: 979 8313620657

Independently Published in Australia

Disclaimer:

This book is intended for informational and inspirational purposes only. It should not be used as a substitute for professional, medical or psychological advice.

Dedicated to
My beloved.
All the lessons life has taught me.
To every soul seeking to reconnect with their true self,
And to all who are brave enough to question their reality.

4

These echoes are not just what we've lived through,
  But what we've silenced.
Listen carefully —
Not every loud thought is true,
And not every quiet one is weak.
— from The Echoes of the Mind

*A*cknowledgments
I would like to extend my heartfelt gratitude to the many people who have supported me throughout this journey—my family, friends, mentors, and readers. Your encouragement, wisdom, and love have been invaluable in helping me complete this journey.

To the authors, thought leaders, and thinkers whose work has influenced me, thank you for being a source of inspiration.

Lastly, to my inner voice, which has guided me through every step of this process, I am eternally grateful. This book would not have been possible without the whispers of my mind reminding me to keep going.

*P*reface

There comes a time—quietly, often without fanfare—when the life we've carefully constructed starts to feel hollow. We go through the motions, meet the expectations, and say all the right things. But somewhere underneath the surface, something stirs. A soft unease. A whisper we can't quite name.

That something is often ourselves.

The parts we've buried, silenced, and edited down so we could survive, fit in, and be accepted. Not because we were weak, but because we were never shown another way.

We live in a world that celebrates noise, speed, and performance. Productivity is praised. Perfection is rewarded. But very few spaces invite us to pause and ask:

"What parts of me have I left behind just to belong here?"

This book was born from that question.

Echoes of the Mind is not a guidebook or a list of affirmations. It's not here to fix you, because you're not broken. You are layered. Shaped by experiences you never fully processed. Carrying stories, you didn't write, but memorized anyway.

We all walk with mental imprints—what I call negative films. Like undeveloped photographs, they carry moments that were never fully seen, never understood, never brought into the light. And yet, they quietly color how we see ourselves, how we move through the world, how we love, fear, and protect.

These imprints don't shout. They echo.

They speak in thought patterns we mistake for truth:

"You're too much."
"You'll never be enough."
"Don't relax—it won't last."
But these thoughts aren't destiny. They are memories.
They're echoes.
And once we learn to recognize them, we can learn to listen differently.

This book is an invitation. Not to "think better" or "be more positive," but to slow down long enough to see the lens you've been looking through. To ask better questions. To pause before the familiar script plays out again.

It's a mirror—one that gently reflects what's always been inside you - your capacity to see clearly, to heal deeply, to come home to yourself.

Inside these pages, you'll find stories, reflections, and questions. You'll explore how your perception has been shaped by old experiences and inherited beliefs. And you'll begin the sacred work of reclaiming your sight—of seeing not through the residue of pain, but through the clarity of presence.

There will be discomfort at times. That's okay.
Discomfort is not failure. It's a doorway.
It means something important is rising.
Something real.
Something is ready to be seen.
So if you've ever felt like you were living a life that didn't quite feel like your own...
If you've ever wondered why the same patterns keep repeating...
If your inner voice has become too loud, too critical, too tired...
You are not alone.

I don't offer these words as an expert, but as someone who has walked this road too. I've questioned my thoughts, doubted my worth, and carried echoes that weren't mine to hold. But I've also learned this:

The answers we seek don't live "out there."
They live in the places we've been most afraid to look.

In the pauses.
In the shadows.
In the echoes.
So, if you're ready to stop performing and start listening—
If you're prepared to meet the self that's been waiting beneath the noise—
Then let's begin.
Together.

7

Table of Contents

Part I: Foundations of the Echo

Chapter 1: Echoes
Where it all begins—the whispers we mistake for truth.

Chapter 2: Elements
The quiet forces that form us, fracture us, and fuel us.

Chapter 3: Vision / Negative Films
Seeing through the lens of memory—undeveloped, distorted, real.

Part II: Confronting the Inner Architecture

Chapter 4: Denied Illusion / Incubation
What we deny doesn't disappear—it gestates. Until we're ready to meet it.

Chapter 5: It's Me (Absorption) - Unity
The unravelling of false selves. The reabsorption of what we left behind.

Chapter 6: Mirrors and Echoes — The Art of Reciprocation, Refraction, and Reflection
What we give. What bends. What comes back? And what we finally see.

Chapter 7: The Perfect Mess — Understanding Functional Dysfunctionality
When the broken becomes normal, and we call it balance.

Part III: Shedding & Returning

Chapter 8: Superficial Living
The masks, the motions, and the cost of staying on the surface.

Chapter 9: Trails of Uncertainty
Walking through fog, learning to trust the step, not the path.

Chapter 10: Befriending Me — The Journey Back to Ourselves
The return. The gentleness. The radical act of meeting yourself again.

Part IV: Integration & Expansion

Chapter 11: Repository Beliefs

The beliefs we didn't choose, but carry as truth, until we question.

Chapter 12: Real-Life Echoes

Other voices. Other echoes. Shared awakenings from the world within.

Chapter 13: The Journey Continues

Healing doesn't end. It evolves. So do we.

8

Echoes

Chapter 1

I recall the transparent, innocent memories of my childhood; they still smell as fresh as ever. Life felt like a canvas just painted—vivid, soft, untouched by expectations. I often catch myself peering through those memory glasses, searching for the inner child who once lived so freely inside me.

But growing up? It doesn't come with a guidebook. Sometimes, it feels like an impossible task. At every turn, questions arise—Why is life so twisted? Why does the world always seem to clash with what feels pure inside? There's a friction between innocence and the so-called "reality" of adulthood, where societal norms often silence our inner truth. What's "right" externally doesn't always sit right within. And in that constant tug of war, something quietly starts to ache.

We don't talk enough about how unbearable those inner collisions can feel. The endless battle between being and becoming. The constant pressure to define what's appropriate, what's acceptable. Who decides that? Why do we judge our own thoughts as if thinking freely isn't our most basic right? Liberation begins in the mind, and yet, we're often the first to shackle ourselves with doubt.

The outside world—its noise, its pressure, its need to define us—can feel like a weight on the soul. The more we absorb, the heavier we become. Until one day, something erupts. Not a dramatic explosion for the world to see, but a quiet volcano inside—self-doubt, self-judgment, unspoken grief. We learn to suppress. To pretend. To move on. Denial becomes our safety net. If we don't look at it, maybe we don't have to deal with it. But volcanoes don't erupt because of the outside—they rupture because of what we've buried too deep for too long.

In the middle of all that emotional noise, a new rush takes over—the desperate need to prove ourselves. To the world. To the mirror. To everyone who ever doubted us. That proving energy runs through us like wildfire, born out of wounds we never paused to heal. We chase

validation, success, and meaning, often without realizing we're running in circles—disconnected from our core.

If we don't pause and tend to the echoes within us, they begin to shape us. They get louder. They become who we are.

Science tells us the average human processes 60,000 to 80,000 thoughts a day—that's nearly 2,500 to 3,300 thoughts every hour. How many of those are truly ours? How many are inherited fears, outdated beliefs, or unconscious echoes of a world that told us who we're supposed to be?

This is why stillness is not a luxury. It's survival. It's healing. It's the most radical thing we can offer ourselves in a world obsessed with noise.

Stillness is not silence—it's clarity. It's sitting with the discomfort and letting it breathe instead of burying it. Let it flow. Don't cling. Don't resist. Observe. Listen. Heal.

It was through lived experience—through love, grief, confusion, and awakening—that I finally began to see how our perceptions shape our entire reality. Life becomes a tangled web of other people's ideas—about success, love, beauty, strength—and in that mess, it's easy to lose our own voice. However, the truth is that we are allowed to pause. We are allowed to question. We are allowed to redefine everything.

We often forget that trusting the process—even when we don't know where it's leading—is our way back to ourselves. Trust means believing we can weather any storm, face our shadows, and rise again.

It means peeling back the layers that never belonged to us in the first place.

Never lose sight of who you are underneath it all. And never stop trusting the messy, beautiful, uncertain journey of self-discovery.

The Everyday Weight We Carry

Not all pain shows up as obvious heartbreak or crisis. Sometimes, it's the soft, quiet thoughts that live in the background—barely noticeable, but always present. These are the micro-echoes. The tiny comparisons we make while scrolling through someone else's highlight reel. The passing glance in the mirror that turns into a silent critique. The nagging inner voice that tells us we're behind, no matter how much we've done. These thoughts don't scream, so we don't label them as harmful. But they gather. They build. And before we realize it, we're walking through our days with a weight that feels normal but was never meant to be carried.

What makes them tricky is how familiar they feel. We don't stop to question them, because they sound like us. But if we slow down, if we're more present, we might notice that many of these thoughts didn't start with us. They were passed down through culture, family, and old experiences that left impressions we never fully processed. Over time, we begin living a version of ourselves shaped more by other people's beliefs than our own truth.

In a world that celebrates constant doing, constant proving, we forget that our minds aren't machines. They're sensitive, layered, and constantly absorbing. And when they're overstimulated, it's not a sign of weakness—it's a sign that they're trying to protect us from too much. However, we don't often give ourselves the permission to pause and check in. To ask: Is this belief even mine? Is this pressure helping me grow, or is it just keeping me stuck?

Stillness can feel foreign—sometimes even scary—because we've been taught to equate quiet with failure. But in reality, stillness is where the truth lives. It's not about shutting everything out. It's about making enough room to hear your own voice again. Not the noise, not the narrative, just you. And healing? It's not always about doing more. Sometimes, it's about doing less—about subtracting

the noise, the habits, the expectations that never belonged to us in the first place.

The Echoes That Enter Through Love

Some of the loudest echoes in our lives come not from pain, but from love—or at least, what we thought love was. They don't always show up through heartbreak or loss. Sometimes it's more subtle. A parent's unmet expectations. A friend who quietly pulled away. A relationship that felt almost right, but never quite enough. These experiences rarely leave visible marks, but they leave a residue. They plant questions that linger inside us: Was I too much? Was I not enough? Why did they pull away?

To protect ourselves, we adapt. We harden. We become more guarded, more cautious. We convince ourselves that needing connection is a weakness. That staying soft makes us naive. So we build armour. We smile while withdrawing. We show strength, even when we're tired of being strong. But over time, that armour becomes its own kind of pain. It keeps us from being hurt, yes—but it also keeps us from being fully seen.

The truth is, most of us weren't taught how to stay open without losing ourselves. We weren't taught that vulnerability isn't about exposure—it's about connection. That it's okay to need, to want, to feel deeply. Real strength isn't in how tightly we hold it all together—it's in how gently we let ourselves come undone. That doesn't mean being reckless with our hearts. It means choosing softness with discernment. Letting love in again—not blindly, but bravely.

Part of healing is forgiving the people who didn't know how to love us. But it's also about forgiving ourselves for the times we didn't know how to choose differently. The echoes that come from love are often the most complex. They carry both warmth and ache. But

they also carry our deepest invitations—to trust, to open, to choose again.

The Unseen Echoes That Shape Us

There's a category of thoughts that don't show up in words. They feel more like reflexes, like habits, like deeply ingrained ways of being. These are the unconscious echoes—the ones we don't even realize we're following. They're not loud. They don't warn us before they show up. They just exist—guiding decisions, shaping reactions, dictating what we avoid and why.

Why do compliments make us flinch? Why do we apologize when we've done nothing wrong? Why do we feel safest in chaos or tension, even when we say we crave peace? These patterns aren't accidents. They're traces of older experiences. Perhaps it was the time when our joy was too loud for someone else to bear. Or when needing help was met with dismissal. Or when love felt conditional on performance, behaviour, or silence. We may not remember the exact moment. But the body does. The heart does.

And because these patterns are quiet and deeply embedded, they often masquerade as truth. They feel natural—even logical. But that's what makes them powerful. We move through life repeating them without question. Until something in us finally asks: Is this really me? Or is this who I became to stay safe?

Awareness is the beginning of everything. Not awareness for the sake of self-criticism, but for liberation. Once we recognize a pattern, we're no longer stuck in it. We get to pause. We get to breathe. We get to decide if it still belongs in our lives.

Healing these unconscious echoes isn't about perfection. It's about curiosity. It's about compassion. It's about letting go of the pressure to "fix" and replacing it with a willingness to feel. To stay present

long enough to make new choices. And eventually, those choices become our new echo—gentler, truer, and ours.

Echoes Within

This chapter was an unknown beginning—one I didn't even feel I needed.

When I first began writing this chapter, I wasn't entirely sure what I was opening. It felt like casually lifting the corner of a rug, only to realize how much dust had been swept underneath for years. I didn't know I was beginning something. I thought I was just expressing a passing thought... but it ended up being a threshold.

This chapter wasn't planned. It wasn't outlined. It came from a strange stillness—the kind that shows up when you're too tired to pretend, and too quiet to distract yourself. And in that stillness, I noticed: my thoughts had become so loud, I had stopped hearing my truth. Or worse—I'd mistaken the noise for truth.

For a long time, I didn't think I needed to go back to my echoes. I thought I was done with them. I believed growth meant moving forward, not looking back. But this chapter showed me something else: that the parts of us we silence don't die—they wait. And sometimes healing doesn't look like fixing anything. Sometimes it looks like finally listening to what you've ignored.

I realized I'd built so much of my identity from defence—trying to be okay, trying to prove something, trying to outrun discomfort. But when I paused... when I let the echoes speak... what came through wasn't weakness or confusion. It was wisdom. Honest, messy, human wisdom I'd been too busy to notice.

If this chapter felt unsettling or strangely familiar to you, good. That means you're waking up to the echoes you didn't know were shaping you, too. Let it happen gently. Don't rush to analyse or

solve the problem. Just sit with it. That marks the beginning of a fundamental transformation.

We don't always know when a new path begins. Sometimes, it's the page we didn't think mattered that opens the whole book.

10

*E*lements

11

Chapter 2

There are moments in life when everything feels fragmented—when something within you is shifting, cracking open, or simply asking to be heard. These are not random disruptions. These are invitations to reconnect with the elements within us that shape our identity, guide our choices, and define how we navigate the world.

Not chemical elements like oxygen or nitrogen, but the intangible ones: memory, longing, grief, hope, connection, belief. These are the real building blocks of our inner world. We carry them not in our hands, but in our hearts, in our breath, and in the silent spaces between our thoughts.

From the first breath we take, we begin to absorb. We're born whole, curious, emotional, and intuitive. Slowly, without realizing it, we begin to collect. Voices. Opinions. Behaviours. Expectations. These become the earliest layers of our inner landscape. They influence how we see the world, how we love, how we define success, and who we believe we are supposed to become.

Over time, these collected elements—many of them inherited or conditioned—begin to crowd out our original voice. The inner static grows louder, and our quiet truth gets buried beneath what the world expects of us.

But buried doesn't mean gone.

Somewhere deep beneath the noise is a quieter self—still intact. Still listening. Still waiting.

This deeper self is what Carl Rogers, the father of Humanistic Psychology, called the "organismic self." It is the real you, unshaped by external conditioning. Rogers believed that the more distance there is between who we truly are and who we think we should be, the more anxiety, sadness, and disconnection we feel. True healing, he said, comes from closing that gap.

Let's explore the elements—emotional, environmental, relational, and volitional—that silently govern our lives.

Emotional Elements – The Inner Weather

Our emotions are not weaknesses. They are data. They are truth-tellers.

In neuroscience, Antonio Damasio's Somatic Marker Hypothesis explains how emotions play a crucial role in informed decision-making. They help us weigh choices, detect danger, and sense alignment or dissonance.

Emotions like joy, grief, envy, awe, or anger are not distractions. They're signals. They whisper:

This boundary matters.

This part of you is aching.

This thing is worth pursuing.

This memory still lingers.

Yet, we live in a culture that rewards composure over honesty, performance over presence. We're often encouraged to silence our discomfort. But the most uncomfortable emotions are usually the most honest ones.

Studies on emotional suppression, as published in the Journal of Personality and Social Psychology, have shown that ignoring or denying emotions can lead to increased stress, poorer memory, and weaker relationships. On the other hand, emotional acceptance increases resilience, clarity, and connection.

What if you didn't label your emotions as "good" or "bad," but simply saw them as part of your internal weather—just clouds passing, each holding a message?

Environmental Elements – The Spaces That Shape Us

Your environment isn't just where you live—it's everything you interact with:

The voices you let in.

The media you consume.

The spaces you avoid.

The energy you allow.

Albert Bandura's Theory of Reciprocal Determinism teaches us that our behaviour, internal state, and environment are constantly influencing one another. Change one, and the others shift too.

That means your environment is either fuelling your authenticity or quietly dimming it.

Ask yourself:

What am I surrounding myself with every day?

Who expands me?

What drains me?

Where do I feel most like myself?

If your environment feels misaligned, don't wait for permission—start curating spaces and connections that reflect the you beneath the noises.

12

Relational Elements – The Mirrors of Self

Relationships are influential teachers. Some show us our light. Others show us our wounds.

According to Attachment Theory (Bowlby), our earliest bonds shape how we relate to intimacy, vulnerability, and love. Suppose we grew up with conditional love or emotional unavailability. In that case, we may carry forward habits of over giving, people-pleasing, or emotional withdrawal.

But the beauty of the human brain is its neuroplasticity—the ability to rewire itself. You are not doomed to repeat what hurt you. You can create new relational templates, not only with others but also with yourself.

And this brings us to the most enduring relationship of all—the one with your inner voice.

What is the tone of that voice?

Does it sound like a critic? A mentor? A forgotten child?

Cognitive Behavioural Therapy (CBT) teaches us that our internal dialogue has immense power. Our thoughts shape our emotions, and our emotions shape our actions. If your self-talk is harsh, your world feels unsafe. If it is gentle and honest, your world begins to soften, too.

The way you speak to yourself becomes the way you navigate everything—from solitude to love to loss.

13

The Element of Choice – The Freedom Within
In the midst of chaos, we forget that one element always remains ours: choice.

Viktor Frankl, psychiatrist and Holocaust survivor, wrote:
"Everything can be taken from a man but one thing: the last of the human freedoms—to choose one's attitude in any given set of circumstances."

Modern neuroscience affirms this. Studies using functional MRI have shown that practices like mindfulness, meditation, and self-reflection activate the brain's prefrontal cortex—the region responsible for intentional decision-making and self-awareness. You can literally strengthen your ability to choose differently.

You may not control the weather of life, but you can always steer your ship. You can decide on your course.

When you begin to leave from this place—when your compass is internal—you shift from reaction to response. From fear to clarity. From proving to being.

Returning to the Original Elements

You are not broken. You are not too late.

You are simply surrounded by layers—noise, pressure, past programming. Beneath all of it, your original elements still exist:

Intuition
Compassion
Inner knowing
Resilience
Curiosity

They may have been buried, but they were never erased.

Your journey isn't about becoming someone new—it's about remembering.

So pause. Breathe.

Whisper -

What am I carrying that isn't mine?

Which elements am I living unconsciously?

What would it feel like to return to the truth of who I was before the world told me who to be?

Because that version of you still lives—quietly, patiently, and powerfully—beneath it all.

Waiting for you to come home.

14

Societal Elements – The Unseen Sculptor

Society is the quiet architect of our inner world—its tools are subtle, yet powerful. It shapes us not only through laws and culture but through unspoken expectations, inherited beliefs, and silent judgment. From the earliest moments of our lives, we begin to receive cues about who we should be, how we should speak, what success looks like, what love should feel like, and who is allowed to belong. We internalize these messages before we even have the language to question them. And so, without realizing it, we begin to craft versions of ourselves that are socially acceptable, digestible, and unthreatening.

We learn to present the "right" kind of face in different rooms. We mute parts of ourselves that feel too raw, too sensitive, too defiant. We choose what's safe over what's true. And often, we mistake acceptance for love, never realizing that a love built on performance is a love that will eventually exhaust us.

But here's the paradox: the same society that conditions us to fit in also gives us the contrast we need to wake up. Every time we feel the ache of not belonging, every time we feel out of place, it's not because something is wrong with us—it's because something deep within us remembers who we are without the masks. These moments of dissonance are sacred. They are not failures, they are signals. They whisper: This isn't your truth.

When we begin to question the structures, we were raised within—whether it's gender norms, cultural taboos, rigid family roles, or societal definitions of worth—we reclaim something vital. We reclaim our voice. We begin to untangle what was given to us from what actually belongs to us. This is the beginning of freedom—not just the external kind, but the inner liberation that comes from living in alignment with your own truth.

Psychologically, this process is echoed in the theory of self-actualization proposed by Abraham Maslow. Once our basic needs
are met, we begin the lifelong journey of becoming who we truly are, beyond societal layers. Similarly, Carl Jung called this "individuation"—the process of integrating all parts of the self, including those rejected by society, to become whole.

And perhaps that is the quiet revolution of our time: choosing to be whole rather than accepted.

So question:

What beliefs am I still carrying because they made me feel safe?

What roles have I outgrown, but still cling to for validation?

And who might I become if I stopped asking for permission to be myself?

The answers won't come all at once. But every time you choose your truth over conformity, you become a little more you. And that is more than enough.

Echoes Within

There was a time I thought life was happening to me. People, moments, decisions—all just swirling around me like weather. But somewhere along the way, I realized: I am part of the weather. I'm not just standing in the storm—I'm shaping it too.

This chapter, Elements, came from my own unlearning. I used to collect everything—people's opinions, expectations, silent judgments—and carry them like I owed them space in my soul. But one day I asked myself, "What if I set it all down? What would be left?"

That question scared me.

But also—it set me free.

This reflection isn't about giving you answers. It's about inviting you to look more gently, more curiously, at the elements shaping your life right now. You don't need to judge them. Just notice. Who are you around when you feel small? What habits feel like armour? Which emotions are asking to be witnessed, not fixed?

And most importantly:

What inside you are still yours, untouched, waiting to be heard?

The world may try to rearrange your pieces, but only you get to decide what stays.

Take this moment.

Lay your hands on your chest.

Breathe.

Feel the ground beneath you.

And ask softly:

What in me is still whole, still true, still mine?

Let that whisper guide you.

15

Vision / Negative Films

16

Chapter 3

Vision is not just what we see with our eyes.

It's how we interpret. How we filter light through layers of memory, belief, bias, and emotional residue. Sometimes, what we mistake for clarity is simply repetition. Sometimes, we're not seeing—we're re-seeing. We're looking at the world through echoes. These are not just ordinary echoes. They are echoes of the mind. They sound like our thoughts. They feel like the truth.

But often, fragments of moments we never fully processed, misunderstood silences, subtle abandonments, small rejections, words that stuck but never healed. I call them negative films—mental imprints never brought to light, still dictating the colour and shape of our present perception. These negatives don't scream. They hum quietly beneath everything.

They whisper:

"You're too much."

"Don't ask."

"Why try? It'll end like last time."

"Love hurts."

"Stay small. It's safer."

We don't remember choosing these beliefs. That's because we didn't.

We absorbed them through reactions, tone, absence, overreactions, and the words left unsaid.

Now they echo inside us, distorting what we see before we even know we're looking.

The Ghosts Behind the Lens

Like photographic negatives, these internal imprints are fragile, easily missed, but powerful.

Left undeveloped, they shape how we define love, trust, power, safety, failure, and self-worth.

A compliment? We dismiss it.

An opportunity? We sabotage it.

A relationship? We doubt it.

A moment of peace? We brace for what might come next.

We believe we're making choices, but often, it's the echo choosing for us.

Many of us walk through life like living archives—carrying emotional negatives we never stopped long enough to develop. They blur the present with old pain, making it hard to trust what's real, let alone what's possible.

And the great tragedy?

We're too busy to notice.

We Want Clarity—but Avoid the Darkroom

Most people are rushing to get things done—chasing goals, checking boxes, being productive. But in the process, they forget to pause.

To see. To develop the emotional photographs of their lives.

I've seen it happen again and again.

In photography galleries, people glide from image to image, drawn to the vibrant, saturated pictures. The colours are loud. Inviting. Easy to talk about.

But then, a black-and-white image appears. And something changes.

They stop. Their bodies still. Their breath softens. A flicker of memory rises. Something unnamed. Something felt. But almost instantly, they move on. Back to the colourful prints. Back to what's digestible. Loud. Safe. Attractive. Because grayscale demands something more.

It demands stillness. Honesty. Presence. It touches something ancient inside us, then dares us to stay long enough to feel it.

But most people don't. They leave before they know why they stopped.

Because the truth? The answers don't always live in colour. They live in the negatives of your soul.

That's where the unspoken resides. That's where the versions of you that never got closure still whisper.

That's where your echoes live—trying to show you the truth you've been too busy or too afraid to develop.

17

Our Vision Is a Memory in Disguise

We assume we're seeing the world as it is. But we're often just seeing it as we were. Our vision is not always fresh. It's not always ours. Most of us see the future through the lens of the past. We mistake old pain for foresight. We mistake trauma for instinct. We mistake silence for strength. We say, "I just know how things go." But no—we're remembering how it felt last time. And we're living from that feeling, not the reality in front of us.

That's how echoes work. They don't move forward. They bounce back.

And they block our sight. We don't see new people—we project old ones onto them. We don't embrace new love—we brace for old hurt.

We don't let ourselves dream—we expect the fall.

Cognitive Lenses & Echo Distortions

To understand how deep this distortion goes, we can turn to two psychological frameworks:

Schema Theory (Piaget, expanded by Beck)

Schemas are mental frameworks created from early experiences.

If you grew up feeling unworthy of affection, you may now view every compliment with suspicion.

Even when surrounded by love, your inner schema whispers: "Don't trust it."

Cognitive Distortions (Beck, Burns)

These are faulty thinking patterns that keep us trapped in echo loops:

Filtering: Focusing only on the negative.

Overgeneralizing: "This always happens to me."
Emotional Reasoning: "I feel like a failure, so I must be one."
Mind Reading: "They must think I'm weak."

Echoes feed distortions. Distortions reinforce schemas. And soon, our inner lens is a loop of old film, blurring the present.

Breaking the Lens

So, how do we see clearly? Not by ignoring the echo, but by developing it. That's what healing is.

Not deleting the past but bringing its negatives into the light.
It looks like:
Naming the first time we felt "not enough."
Writing down the thought and tracing it back.
Asking: Whose voice is this? Is it mine?
Asking: What would someone without this belief see right now?

It's not about forced positivity. It's about clarity. Seeing things as they are, not as we were. It's about curiosity. Not controlled. It's about slowly, tenderly cleaning the lens. Because when we do, we realize:

We're not broken. We're just looking through old film. We don't need to be someone else. We just need to see ourselves—clearly, truly, finally.

Seeing With My Own Eyes

There was a time when I thought my fear was wisdom. I thought my hesitation was discernment. I mistook my echoes for intuition. I believed I was seeing things clearly—being realistic, being careful—but I was really living from old wounds. I didn't trust praise because deep down I feared it wouldn't last. I didn't allow ease because the echo said, "Ease always ends."

I believed I was being self-aware, but I was really being self-protective. Then something shifted. I began to ask better questions. I started to wonder: Are these thoughts mine—or are they inherited? I looked inward, sat with the "black and white" pictures of my past—the moments I used to skip, the memories I used to rush through. I found meaning in the quiet. I stopped reacting automatically and started noticing more. I heard silence differently.

I gave weight to the jolt in my chest when something old tried to speak. And slowly, I began to see—not through fear or history, but through presence. Now, I still have echoes. But I know they are echoes. I don't let them speak for me anymore. I sit with them, I listen, and then I move forward with clearer eyes.

Because the answer doesn't live in the noise. It lives in the pause. It lives in the shadow. And I'm finally learning to see.

Denied Illusion / Incubation

18

Chapter 4
There are thoughts we speak aloud.
There are thoughts we silence.
And then, there are thoughts caught somewhere between truth and fear—seeds left to incubate in the shadowy corners of our mind.

These are the thoughts we're not ready to face. The truths we deny, whether because we fear their consequences or because someone else denied them for us. Sometimes the world says, "No, you can't say that, feel that, want that." And sometimes, we say it to ourselves. Either way, something inside retreats—not gone, just buried beneath layers of silence.

That is where incubation begins.

What Is Incubation of the Self?

Incubation here is not the fertile pause before growth. It is a holding cell, a limbo where unprocessed truths and emotions dwell—sometimes for months, years, or even decades. It begins with a small refusal: "I can't deal with this now." "No one will understand." "I shouldn't feel this way." These responses seem like shields, but in truth, they delay healing and invite distortion.

The longer a thought or feeling stays unexamined, the more it mutates. It starts to whisper illusions:

"I'm not worthy."

"This is just who I am."

"Nothing will ever change."

We don't just carry these thoughts; we become them.

When Denial Comes

19

Illusion slips in through two doors:
External denial: When society, family, culture, or a person invalidates your truth.

Self-denial: When you internalize that invalidation and silence your own voice.

At first, denying feels easier. Escaping discomfort can feel like relief, like a much-needed breath. You convince yourself: "I'm fine." But the mind knows when it's lying, and the body always remembers.

This denial is slow erosion, a quiet unmaking of self.

The Dangerous Comfort of Illusion

At first, the incubated truth is a soft murmur—a confusion, a restless ache. But over time, it hardens into a corrosive voice inside, telling you who you are, what you deserve, what you cannot become. You live inside that echo. And the longer it remains unchallenged, the more it calcifies into illusion.

That illusion becomes an identity. It quietly governs your actions, your self-perception, and your relationships.

"I am unlovable."

"I am not enough."

"No one understands me."

These are not truths, but they feel true, because we've carried them so long.

The Point of No Return?

20

There comes a quiet, terrifying moment when you realize you've gone too far from yourself. You don't remember who you were before the mask. You no longer know which thoughts are truly yours. The echo has become your only voice.

This moment can feel like a point of no return. As if the real self is lost forever, buried beneath years of silence, suppression, and illusion.

And it's true—some versions of us may never come back. But healing is not about going back.

Healing is about building forward—gently, slowly—from wherever you are. It's about recognizing the echoes inside and asking:

Does this still serve me?

Is this mine to carry?

The Psychological Journey of Harmful Incubation

This journey often moves through stages:

Avoidance: You suppress or deny what you feel or know.

Discomfort: You feel inner conflict but push it away.

Adaptation: You adjust your identity to fit the illusion.

Attachment: You defend the illusion, telling yourself it's your story.

Disconnection: You lose touch with your authentic self. The echo becomes your reality.

This is why many feel like strangers to themselves—they've incubated illusions so long that the real self no longer feels familiar.

Why Illusions Are Addictive

Illusions are more than lies. They are anaesthetics. They numb the ache, distract from grief, and offer momentary peace amid chaos.

But at what cost?

We stop living our true lives. We forget our original rhythm. We trade meaning for the comfort of stability.

And in that forgetting, purpose fades quietly.

The Soul Knows When We Betray It

There is a soul-level grief from self-abandonment that can't be silenced. It lives in subtle ways—in unexplained anxiety, in chronic fatigue, in a constant, restless ache.

The soul knows when we deny ourselves. It whispers beneath the noise: You were made for more than this.

The Science of the Silent Echo

Neuroscience reveals how chronic emotional suppression shapes us:

The amygdala, the brain's fear centre, becomes overactive, heightening anxiety and stress.

The prefrontal cortex, responsible for Reasoning and decision-making, weakens, making it harder to think clearly or regulate emotions.

Prolonged denial stresses the body, weakening immune function and increasing the risk of illness.

This isn't just psychological—it's biological. The mind and body are inextricably linked. What we bury inside does not stay buried without consequence.

Choosing to Listen: The Sacred Work of Healing

Healing is not fixing what's broken. It is remembering who you were before the noise of denial.

It means reclaiming those incubated thoughts, those silent echoes, and holding them up to the light. Asking:

Is this mine?

Is this still true?

This act alone is revolutionary.

A healed mind is not just peaceful—it's powerful. It sees clearly, chooses intentionally, and breaks the cycle of inherited harm.

Why Healing Changes Everything

When one person heals, they change the echo they send into the world. They create space for others to do the same. Transformation becomes contagious.

Healing rewrites the story—not just for ourselves, but for everyone we meet.

If you want to start somewhere, here are some starting points, and you will draw the finish line by yourself.

What beliefs or thoughts have you carried silently for years?

Which of them truly belongs to you, and which are echoes of someone else's fear or expectation?

What part of you is currently incubating—waiting for expression, but still waiting for permission?

How might your life change if you began to listen to that part?

When we stop denying our inner lives, we begin to write a truer story. And from that story, a different future becomes possible—not just for us, but for everyone who hears our echo.

Let that be your echo.

Echoes Within

Writing this chapter felt like looking into a mirror I hadn't wanted to face before. There's something about admitting how much we hide from ourselves—those quiet parts that get tucked away because they feel too scary, too messy, or just not allowed. For me, realizing how denial and incubation live inside all of us was both unsettling and freeing.

We live in a world that often tells us to keep going, to push through, to fix things fast. It rarely makes space for the slow, uncomfortable process of sitting with what's hard to say or even to feel. But I've come to see that this "incubation" isn't just some stuck moment—it's a secret place where real change can start, if we're brave enough to listen.

At the same time, I know how easy it is to get trapped there, to let those hidden thoughts become the story we tell ourselves about who we are. And that's heartbreaking.

So, this chapter is really an invitation to be kinder to ourselves, to gently shine a light on those buried truths, and to start asking: which parts of this story are really mine? And which parts have I just accepted because someone else said so?

I wrote this because I want you to feel less alone. We all carry these echoes inside, sometimes for years. But we also have the strength to meet them, understand them, and begin to heal.

Thank you for being here, for reading, and for trusting this journey. I hope you find a little more space inside yourself to listen and to heal.

21

It's Me (Absorption) - Unity

22

Chapter 5

Imagine yourself standing alone in a dark room.

It's quiet—too quiet. The kind of silence that presses in from all sides, heavy and intimate. The air feels dense, the floor beneath you cold and uneven. You reach out, but your hands meet only shadows. You don't know exactly how you got here, but you see this space intimately. This room is not just a place—it's a feeling. A pause. A reckoning.

As your eyes begin to adjust, you look down and see that the floor is covered in puzzle pieces—scattered, mismatched, broken. Some are sharp and jagged, others smooth but faded. These are fragments of you: memories, emotions, beliefs, wounds, triumphs—every piece of your life, broken apart by time, trauma, joy, and everything in between.

You don't know where to start. But somewhere inside, a spark stirs—a small but steady courage. You bend down, pick up a piece, and feel its weight in your hand. It's not about collecting everything all at once. It's about choosing—gently, carefully—what deserves to come back with you.

This room, dark and quiet, is where self-absorption begins. But not the kind you've been warned about. This is not ego or selfishness. This is the sacred kind. The kind that happens when life slows down—or knocks you down—and you finally turn inward. Here, you absorb everything you've been running from: your pain, your joy, your shame, your resilience.

You are alone, but not abandoned.

You are surrounded by everything you've ever been.

23

The Dark Room: Absorption Begins

Self-absorption, in this moment, is simply seeing. Picking up the pieces. Sitting with them. Feeling them without judgment.

Some pieces are easy to hold—snapshots of joy, of feeling seen, of being loved. Others sting—the jagged edges of heartbreak, failure, or rejection. There is no order to it. No clear map. Just you and the fragments.

But picking them up isn't enough.

Because if you only absorb without sorting, without understanding, the weight of those pieces can crush you. They can cut you. They can keep you stuck in the dark.

That's where integration comes in.

Integration is when you begin to understand the pieces. When you stop simply gathering and start building. You try to fit things together—not to make a perfect picture, but to make one that makes sense to you. Slowly, deliberately, you begin to reconstruct yourself.

As you work, a soft light begins to grow in the room. Piece by piece, the shape of you starts to return—not as you were, but as you are now.

24

What Draws Us into the Dark Room

Sometimes life throws us into this place—through grief, loss, burnout, rejection. Other times, we walk in by choice, seeking stillness, needing truth.

The trigger doesn't always matter. What matters is that once you're here, you're faced with a decision: Will I pick up the pieces? Will I face what I've hidden? Will I give myself permission to change?

And here's the most challenging part—some of those pieces are not meant to return.

You'll find old beliefs that whisper, "I'm not enough," or "I always mess things up," or "I don't deserve love." You've carried them for so long, they almost feel like home. But they're not. They're weight you no longer need to take.

And healing means having the courage to set them down.

How Absorption Can Heal or Harm

Self-absorption can be a gift when we use it to listen to ourselves, to feel deeply, to reconnect with what's been lost. But without care, it can become a spiral. We get stuck turning over the same painful piece, again and again, without ever understanding where it belongs—or if it belongs at all.

That's when self-awareness becomes self-punishment.

That's when feeling becomes drowning.

Integration is what saves us.

It's the voice inside that says: I see this pain. I honour this memory. I acknowledge this part of me, but I choose how it shapes me moving forward.

It's not erasing. It's not pretending. It's deciding.

The Puzzle of You: The Work of Integration

Integration is not quick. It's not always graceful. Sometimes you try to fit a piece into your new picture and realize it doesn't belong. Other times, you find one you thought was lost—something bright and powerful that reminds you of who you were before the world told you to shrink.

It's a deeply personal process. You ask yourself:

Does this belief serve me?

Is this memory a lesson or a wound?

Do I want this story to shape the next chapter of my life?

With every answer, you place another piece.

And with every piece, the light grows stronger. The dark room begins to shift. You start to see not just the puzzle, but the mosaic. Not perfect—but unmistakably yours.

25

Unity: Becoming Whole Again
    Eventually, something beautiful happens.
You see yourself, not in brokenness, but in wholeness. A self that contains everything you've lived through and still stands. Not because you've healed everything, but because you've chosen to be with yourself in the healing.

This is unity.

Unity is the feeling of being on your own side again. Of knowing you don't have to keep proving or performing. You're not a project to fix. You're a person to love.

From this place, decisions become easier. Life feels more spacious. You can say yes without guilt and no without fear. You trust yourself again—not perfectly, but deeply.

The Power of Choice: What You Leave Behind

You don't have to carry every piece.

In fact, real healing comes when you let go. When you set aside what no longer fits—old fears, other people's opinions, outdated versions of yourself. You are not obligated to hold onto pain just because it shaped you.

Integration gives you the power to decide what you want to carry forward.

You are the curator of your soul.

Choose the pieces that make you feel alive.

My Own Dark Room

Writing this chapter brought me back.

I've been in that dark room. Many times. I know what it's like to kneel on that cold floor, overwhelmed by memories, fears, and questions I didn't have the answers to. I know the silence. I know the weight.

But I also know the spark.

I remember the moment I picked up my first piece—not because I was brave, but because I had nothing left to lose. I kept going, one shard at a time. And slowly, I began to recognize myself again.

The process is never perfect. But it's always worth it.

So if you're in your dark room right now, I want to say this: You're not lost. You're just gathering.

Be gentle. Be curious. And trust that the light is coming—not from outside, but from within.

Because at the end of the day, it's always been you. Your story. Your voice. Your hands, steady and soft, putting yourself back together.

You are not broken. You are becoming your being.

Thank you for walking this part of the path with me. Keep going. The next piece is waiting.

26

Mirrors and Echoes — The Art of Reciprocation, Refraction, and Reflection

27

Chapter 6

There are moments in life when we speak, act, or give—and then pause, waiting. We wait for a sign, a word, a gesture in return. Something. Anything. It's a quiet kind of hoping, a longing for reciprocation.

But when it doesn't come, something inside us falters.

We start to question ourselves. Did they not hear me? Did it not matter? Did I not matter?

The Need for Reciprocation: Looking for Ourselves in Others

We're wired to seek connection. To feel seen, heard, and valued. It's human. But sometimes that yearning becomes a dependence. We start tying our sense of worth to how others respond—or don't.

We want others to echo our efforts, to validate our feelings, to confirm that what we're doing is right.

Why?

Because when we are not fully content—when we have unmet needs, inner wounds, or unfulfilled expectations—we naturally reach outward. We look to others, especially those closest to us, to do what we haven't yet done for ourselves: to soothe, to heal, to complete us.

And when they don't, we react. We blame. We withdraw. We lash out. Or worse, we go quiet.

But these reactions aren't really about them. They are reflections of what's missing within us. Reciprocation becomes a mirror—and the absence of it, a painful spotlight on our own unmet needs.

28

Reflection: What the World Shows Us Is Often What We Hide from Ourselves

There's a saying: when you point one finger at someone, four are pointing back at you. It's cliché, but it's true.

When we feel let down by the world, when someone doesn't respond the way we hoped, it can be a powerful cue to look inward.

What am I really needing here?

What am I expecting them to give me that I haven't given to myself?

Am I looking for love, approval, security—from outside, instead of creating it within?

We often forget that every relationship, every interaction, every disappointment is a reflection. It shows us what still aches. What still feels incomplete? And if we're willing to look gently and honestly, we'll see that the frustration isn't about them. It's about what's waiting to be healed inside us.

Refraction: When the Image Warps

But reflection isn't always clean and clear. Sometimes, even when we try to look within, the image is blurred, twisted, distorted, or out of focus.

This is refraction.

Refraction happens when light bends. When what we see isn't quite what's real. In life, refraction happens when our perception is bent by unhealed pain, old stories, or layers of emotional dust that have built up over time.

And this distortion doesn't just affect how we see others—it clouds how we see ourselves.

We look in the mirror and don't recognize the person staring back. Not because we've changed physically, but because we've lost touch with who we are beneath the noise and reaction.

We try to wipe the mirror clean—change our behaviour, our routines, maybe even our circle—but forget that the dust has settled on us, too. If we don't clear the debris from within, the reflection will always be unclear, no matter how much we polish the glass.

The Silent Inheritance: Passing Down Refractions

There's something else about refraction—it doesn't stay contained.

When we don't tend to our own distortions, they ripple outward. We pass them on—often unconsciously—to the people closest to us. To our partners, our children, and our friends. To the next generation.

Our pain becomes their atmosphere. Our silence becomes their confusion. Our unresolved patterns become their lessons.

That's the quiet danger of not doing our inner work. But here's the quiet power, too: when we begin to heal, to reflect clearly, to choose conscious reciprocation, that also gets passed on.

Healing is contagious. So is self-awareness.

29

Breaking the Cycle: From Outer Noise to Inner Clarity

So what do we do when we realize we've been chasing reflections in others? When we notice that our expectations are rooted in what we haven't yet given ourselves?

We pause. We breathe. We turn inward.

Instead of demanding reciprocity from the world, we begin to ask:

What do I need to give myself right now?

What am I asking someone else to validate that I haven't validated myself?

We stop reacting and start reflecting—with gentleness. We get curious about our pain instead of being ashamed of it. We listen to our inner echoes and learn to respond with compassion, not criticism.

And we remember that the most powerful form of reciprocation comes not from others, but from ourselves.

Reciprocation as Self-Compassion

What would happen if, the next time we felt unheard or unseen, we didn't spiral outward—but turned toward ourselves instead?

What if, in the space where we usually wait for someone else's response, we responded to ourselves with love, kindness, and affirmation?

That is real reciprocity: giving back to ourselves what we keep trying to outsource.

When we meet our own needs, we stop grasping. We stop resenting. We start relating from wholeness, not from hunger.

30

From Reflection to Truth: Seeing Yourself Clearly

As we clean the mirror—from the inside out—we begin to see ourselves clearly again.

We remember who we are beneath the disappointments, beyond the warped reflections. And from that clarity comes peace.

Not perfection. Not controlled. But peace—a grounded, honest relationship with who we are. A willingness to be with ourselves, even in uncertainty. A soft confidence that says: I don't need to chase your echo to know my voice.

My Own Warped Mirror

I've spent years looking for reflections in others—years hoping someone would mirror back something I couldn't quite hold myself. Approval. Belonging. Enough-ness.

But every time that reflection didn't show up, it hurt. I blamed them. I blamed life. But eventually, I had to ask: what was I really seeking? And why wasn't I giving it to myself?

It wasn't easy. My own mirror had become cloudy, blurred by self-doubt, comparison, and fear. But slowly, gently, I began to clean it. I stopped expecting others to reflect my worth and started seeing it in myself. Not all at once. Piece by piece.

And that changed everything.

If you're feeling unseen or unheard right now, I want to offer this: Maybe the world isn't ignoring you. Maybe it's pointing you inward.

Maybe it's time to stop waiting for the echo and start becoming the source.

31

You are not broken.
You're refracted.
And once you see that, you can begin the most beautiful journey of all—not back to the world, but back to yourself.

32

The Perfect Mess — Understanding Functional Dysfunctionality

33

Chapter 7

It's late at night. The lights are off, the room is quiet, and you're lying there wondering why your life, which seems "fine" on the surface, feels slightly offbeat. You go to work, meet people, and perform routines. Everything looks okay. But deep inside, something's off. It doesn't hurt sharply, but it hums like a low, stubborn frequency in the background of your mind.

That, right there, is functional dysfunctionality.

It doesn't scream. It whispers.

It doesn't break down. It bends.

And yet, in its subtle way, it holds us together.

What Is Functional Dysfunctionality?

Functional dysfunctionality is the paradox of something working while being, at its core, broken or misaligned. It's the façade of functionality held up by systems, people, and emotions that have cracks—some visible, some invisible.

It's when your life still moves, even if every part of it limps a little.

It's when a person smiles while battling depression.

It's when a society claims to be progressive, but still silently breeds inequality.

It's when relationships go on, even when both hearts feel unheard.

Dysfunction doesn't always mean collapse. Sometimes, it's the very thing keeping the shaky structure from falling apart. Like old glue holding together fragile pieces of a forgotten vase, dysfunction fills the gaps we don't know how to fix yet.

And strangely... it works.

Why Dysfunction Seems So Functional

We think of dysfunction as a flaw. But what if it's more than that? What if it's an adaptive response—our inner self doing its best to cope, compensate, or hold on?

Our mind adapts to chaos by creating rhythms within it. A person who's always in emotional distress might develop an impeccable sense of humour to survive. A child growing up in a dysfunctional household might become hyper-aware, people-pleasing, highly perceptive—all as a way to manage unpredictability.

These are functional responses to dysfunctional settings.

They don't "fix" the environment, but they help us live within it.

So dysfunction glues together the semi-functional parts of our identity. It fills the hollow spaces. Without it, we'd fall apart. We'd keep searching for suitable fillers to make life seem bearable.

We are not alone in this.

We live among people stitched together with silent screams and invisible fatigue.

We live in a society that sells perfection but thrives on quiet disorder.

We praise functionality in systems that are rotting at the core.

And yet, life goes on.

34

The Functional Society Built on Dysfunction

Take a look around. A person stuck in traffic, scrolling through anxiety reels on their phone. A couple arguing over dishes because neither of them feels emotionally safe. An office full of people trying to meet deadlines they don't believe in. A family where no one talks about grief, but everyone carries it silently.

It's all working. People are moving, buying, selling, and speaking.

But look closely and you'll see the dysfunction: in mindsets, in communication, in the gaps between expectation and reality.

We build beliefs out of pain.

We normalize behaviours born of trauma.

We inherit patterns that don't belong to us but shape us anyway.

Our structures—governments, relationships, communities—are built to look functional. But underneath, there are endless loopholes, unspoken truths, crooked ideologies, failed explorations, and broken expectations.

And yet... there's beauty in this imperfection.

The Beauty of Imperfection

We are not meant to be perfect. We are not machines.

The cracks in us allow space for curiosity, for questions, for longing.

Our dysfunctions don't just create chaos—they give birth to wisdom, art, innovation, and empathy.

Functional depression is one of the quietest and most dangerous forms of this. When someone laughs in public but breaks in private.

When they meet every deadline but feel dead inside. When their soul is starving, but no one notices because their smile is always ready.

They function. But they're drowning.

They show up. But they're exhausted.

And no one sees the cost.

This dysfunction teaches us something vital: we must pay attention not just to what works, but how and why it works.

A Personal Memory: The Dinner Table

I remember sitting at a dinner table one evening, years ago. A room full of laughter. Family members are talking over each other. The smell of food. The clinking of plates. Everything looked perfect.

But beneath that table was a battlefield.

Unspoken grief. Misunderstood emotions. Years of resentment were buried under politeness. It worked—we all came together. We passed the salt. We complimented the food. But it was dysfunctional, deeply.

That dinner became a metaphor for my life for many years. Outwardly fine. Inwardly fractured.

It took years to realize that the dysfunction was a kind of language. A way of surviving. And the moment I began to understand it, it started losing its grip. I began to ask why certain reactions were repeating. Why certain emotions returned, no matter how much I tried to outgrow them.

And that's when healing began.

The Evil Within: When Dysfunction Crosses the Threshold

There's a shadow side to this, too.

When dysfunction is left unexamined, it grows.

It breeds bitterness, envy, cynicism, and self-sabotage.

It turns into quiet hatred—for the world, for others, for ourselves.

That's when the evil inside us awakens—not the kind of evil we see in stories, but a more subtle one:

The one that stops us from trusting anyone.

The one who enjoys someone else's failure.

The one that pushes love away before it can leave us.

The one that lies, not to deceive others, but to protect our own fragile story.

This is what happens when the pain of dysfunction reaches the boiling point.

But here's the hope: it can also be the threshold of transformation.

Reconnecting: Healing Through Awareness

The only way out is through.

We must walk back through the dysfunction—see it, feel it, name it. Reconnect with the parts of ourselves we abandoned to survive. Recognize the good and the evil, not to shame one or glorify the other, but to understand them.

Because only when we shine light on our shadows do they begin to lose power.

Dysfunction gifted us these realizations.

It broke us just enough to become curious.

It confused us just enough to make us wiser.

It exhausted us just enough to make rest feel like resurrection.

And when we look at ourselves clearly, in all our messy, torn, beautiful fragments, we see the truth: we are not broken. We are becoming.

The Privilege of Seeing Clearly

We are privileged—not because our lives are perfect—but because we've been given the ability to see. To witness this paradox. To name the mess. To find beauty in what shouldn't work, but does. To be human, not in spite of dysfunction, but because of it.

When we finally see ourselves with the naked eye—not filtered through expectations or projections—something sacred happens.

We stop trying to fix everything and start understanding it.

We forgive our imperfections.

We thank our survival strategies.

We begin to gently shape a new kind of functionality—one that doesn't hide the cracks, but honours them.

Because if everything worked perfectly, we'd never learn.

We'd never imagine.

We'd never feel the need to understand others or ourselves.

Dysfunction is not failure.

It is the beginning of something real.

There was a time I believed that something had gone terribly wrong with me. I couldn't understand why I kept ending up in the same cycles—why certain relationships drained me, why some emotions came back like echoes, or why I felt so alone even in rooms filled with love.

It took me years to realize I wasn't broken. I was simply responding to a reality that never gave me the tools to understand myself fully.

Looking back, I now see that every "dysfunction" in me was actually a call—an invitation to stop, to listen, and to unravel the noise I had inherited. I had been taught to keep moving, to stay strong, to hold myself together even if I was bleeding internally. I wore strength like armour, but beneath it was a child—confused, sensitive, trying to breathe.

Writing this chapter was not easy. It asked me to revisit moments I've tried to forget. Moments when I judged myself for not being "enough." Moments when I lashed out, not because I was cruel, but because I didn't know how to express what was aching inside me. Moments when I sat in silence, hoping someone would notice I wasn't okay.

But here's what I've learned: dysfunction is part of the design, not as a punishment, but as a mirror. It holds up our truth when we're too scared to speak it aloud. It holds up our longing, our pain, and our unspoken questions. And most of all, it offers us a doorway. A doorway back to ourselves.

We're all a little dysfunctional. We all carry hidden bruises. But that doesn't make us any less worthy. In fact, it makes us more real.

So if you, dear reader, find yourself caught in chaos or confusion, I want you to know—it's okay. Your soul isn't malfunctioning. You're just being reshaped. Trust that.

Let your dysfunction speak to you. Let it show you what you've hidden. Let it point you back to your truth, not the one you perform for the world, but the one you quietly long to live.

Because in this strange and imperfect life, maybe dysfunction isn't what breaks us.

Maybe it's what brings us home.

35

Superficial Living

36

Chapter 8
Living on the Surface

We live fast. We live loud. We live on display.

Every morning, the first thing we see isn't the sunrise or the warmth of sunlight on our skin—it's the cold glow of a screen. We swipe, scroll, tap, and like—often before we even see ourselves in the mirror. There's something quietly tragic about how quickly we reach out for something outside of us before we look within.

The world feels more connected than ever, but inside, many of us think more fractured and alone. Superficial living isn't just a byproduct of modern life—it's become the rhythm of it. We dress up emptiness with aesthetics and call distraction "living."

But... when was the last time you sat in complete silence without trying to escape it?

The Performance of Existence

We put on costumes made of curated moments. There's this unspoken pressure to look put together—happy, prosperous, whole—even when inside, we feel like we're unravelling.

We text people we barely feel close to. We post smiles that don't reach our eyes. We hide real tears behind productivity and schedule joy for "later."

We confuse being watched with being truly seen.

It's easier to skim the surface than to dive into the messy, unpredictable ocean of our feelings. The surface is safe, but nothing real grows there.

Why Stay on the Surface?

Because going deeper asks a lot from us. Presence. Honesty. Surrender.

Superficiality feels comfortable, especially in a world that rewards how things look, not how they feel. But comfort isn't peace. Silence isn't always calm—it can be the noise we've shoved inside.

We settle for temporary fixes. We scroll to numb out. Shop to feel worthy. Stay busy to avoid the questions that might break open the identities we've built so carefully.

But your soul always knows.

It whispers in restlessness, in midnight anxiety, in that strange emptiness—even on your "good" days. That whisper is not dysfunction. It's a message you keep muting.

When the Universe Whispers—and Then Shouts

The universe has a rhythm. It doesn't knock once and leave—it repeats. It sends soft nudges when you drift off course. But if you don't listen, it brings storms.

The lessons you avoid don't disappear. They come back louder, harsher, until something breaks—until your world shakes just enough to push you inward.

This isn't punishment. It's alignment.

Anything hollow—whether a relationship without depth, a job without meaning, or a life lived just for show—eventually crumbles. It was never meant to carry the weight of your soul.

Living or Just Existing?

There's a kind of living where you breathe but don't really feel. Days pass without touching you. Conversations happen, but don't reach your heart.

You might look fine on the outside, but inside there's a quiet ache whispering: Something is missing.

This is the cost of superficial living. It disconnects you from yourself. Locks you in a prison with invisible walls. You look okay, sound okay, but you feel like a stranger in your own life.

And no one can free you from that prison but you.

The Soul's Memory

We came here alone and will leave alone. What stays isn't the possessions, the applause, or the impressions—it's the truth, the tenderness, the moments we showed up for ourselves.

The universe expands by creating, shedding, and becoming. You are no different. You weren't made to live on the surface or in silence. You weren't sent here to decorate a mask.

You were born to peel away everything that's not you.

37

Breaking the Surface

Reclaiming yourself isn't loud—it's quiet, slow, and deeply intentional. It's choosing to watch the sunrise without feeling the need to capture it. It's letting a song break you open, letting it move through you without resistance. It's sitting alone in a café for an hour, letting time pass without the interruption of a glowing screen. It's saying "I don't know" and meaning it, choosing honesty over the performance of certainty. It's truly listening when someone speaks, not planning your reply, but being fully there. It's turning off the noise, even when the silence feels uneasy. It's touching the earth with bare feet and remembering—viscerally—that you are human, and that this moment is all that's needed.

Breaking the surface rarely looks grand. Often, it's found in the smallest, quietest pauses. Picture this: you're in a café. Life hums around you—baristas calling names, keyboards clicking, conversations overlapping. You're scrolling, barely present. Then, the light shifts. It catches your coffee cup. You notice the steam, the warmth of the ceramic in your hands. You pause. Just for a second, the world softens—and you are here. Fully.

That small moment? It's sacred. Not because it's perfect, but because it's real. This is what it means to return to yourself—not through spectacle, but through presence, not through doing more, but through being more awake to what already is.

38

The Mirror Speaks
Sometimes the mirror doesn't lie—it reminds.

It reflects not just how we look, but whether we're present in our own lives. You can't fake being whole in your own reflection. You either see yourself or the version of you trying to hold it all together.

Ask yourself: Who's living your life right now? The real you, or the edited you?

And if you feel distant from yourself—if your inner voice has grown faint—that's okay.

That's the beginning of coming back.

I Know This Place

If you've made it this far, something in you is stirring—a quiet nudge, a soft pull inward. Maybe it's a longing you haven't fully named yet. Maybe it's the ache that's been with you for a while, hidden beneath routines and roles and all the noise we've grown used to. Whatever it is, it matters. Because it means you're ready to return. Not to some perfect version of yourself, not to a polished idea of who you think you should be, but to you. The real you. The one who feels deeply. The one who's tired of pretending. The one who's been waiting for the permission to come home to yourself.

You're not alone in this. So many of us are aching beneath the surface, silently desperate to be known, to be whole, to be real. We no longer need to suffer from our pain. We can sit with it. Hold it gently. Let it teach us, soften us, reshape us.

Let this be your reminder:

You're not here to be perfect.

You're not here to impress or perform.

You're here to be whole.

And wholeness doesn't live in the noise, in the scrolling, in the striving—it lives in the quiet spaces. The ones we often avoid because they feel too still, too raw, too honest. But that's exactly where the light is.

I know this place because I've lived there too. I've spent years behind masks—smiling when I was aching, saying I was fine when I was unravelling. I chased goals that didn't matter to me, just to feel worthy. I filled the silence with distractions because I was scared of what it might reveal. But when the universe stopped whispering and started shaking me awake, I had no choice but to listen. The numbness cracked open. The fog cleared just enough for me to hear the voice I'd buried: Come back to me.

This chapter—these words—are part of that return. Writing them is how I found my way back to my own breath, my own truth. And if something in you is waking up too, if you feel the pull to go deeper, I want you to know: you're not broken. You're being called home.

So take the risk. Turn down the noise. Sit with what's real. Go beneath the surface.

Because your soul has been waiting, and it has never once given up on you.

Trails of Uncertainty

39

Chapter 9

Life doesn't move in straight lines. It weaves. It backtracks. Sometimes it stalls altogether. We crave clarity, but what we get is often ambiguity. And instead of welcoming it, we try to fix it, label it, push through it, or avoid it entirely. However, the truth is that the most important moments in life—the ones that truly change us—often begin in uncertainty.

We've been taught to fear not knowing. To be unsure is often equated with weakness. So we scramble for answers, certainty, blueprints. But what if not knowing isn't the problem? What if it's the beginning of something sacred?

In reality, uncertainty is not an enemy. It's an invitation. It's the space between who we've been and who we are becoming. It's where transformation begins.

The Illusion of Certainty

Modern life conditions us to believe everything should be mapped out. We're expected to have a five-year plan by the time we're twenty. We're supposed to know who we are, what we want, and where we're headed—early, loudly, and definitively. There's no room for pausing. No permission to wander.

However, certainty is often just an illusion masquerading as confidence. It's comforting, yes. But it's also limiting. It builds walls around what's possible.

We want life to work like a camera on auto-focus—fast, clear, optimized. But that's not how growth works. Real life is more like manual mode. It requires you to slow down, adjust the focus yourself, observe the light, and even accept when the frame is a bit off-centre.

Our obsession with knowing keeps us from seeing. We're so focused on the final picture that we miss the raw, unfiltered beauty of the process.

The Camera Roll

Consider your phone's camera roll for a moment.

How many photos do you have saved right now? Thousands? Maybe tens of thousands? We capture sunsets, food, coffee cups, our faces—over and over. But how many of those moments did we actually experience?

Here's the irony: the more we document life, the more detached we often become from it.

You go to a concert and instinctively pull out your phone. You zoom, adjust, record, and maybe even switch angles. But in doing all of that, you miss the actual feeling of the music vibrating through your body. The phone saw it—but did you?

We are so obsessed with getting the perfect shot that we forget to live in the moment. Our eyes are trained to look through lenses instead of with presence. We're trying to curate proof of our lives instead of living them.

And just like with cameras, we treat uncertainty like something to edit out. But the truth is, it's often the blurry, unfiltered moments that end up meaning the most.

40

The Journey Isn't a Straight Line

The path you're on right now may not look like what you expected. It might feel chaotic or aimless. You may be second-guessing choices, questioning your identity, and wondering if you're falling behind. But the detours are often where life begins to reveal what really matters.

There is a misconception that letting go means losing. That surrender is failure. But letting go isn't about giving up. It's about loosening your grip on what isn't real. It's about finally giving space for what is.

When we stop trying to force clarity, we make space for deeper understanding. When we allow uncertainty to exist without labelling it a problem, we open ourselves to insight.

I remember sitting alone late at night, the cold glow of my iPhone screen cutting through the dark room, scrolling through photos I barely recognized—smiling faces frozen in time, moments carefully framed but somehow distant. A vacation where I spent more time capturing the perfect shot than actually feeling the sun on my skin. I felt a strange ache, unsure if I was longing for a past that never really was or just exhausted from never fully showing up in the present. And then there was the moment after my father died, when I was supposed to be strong, managing calls, condolences, the endless social expectations—but inside, I didn't know what to feel. No grief, no relief, just numbness. I cried at the wrong times, smiled when I wanted to scream. It was confusing and messy, but deeply human. In those moments, the idea of certainty felt like a cruel joke. Life wasn't neat or scripted. It was raw, unpredictable, and painful—and that was okay.

It's easy to romanticize certainty, but it rarely leads to the kind of richness that comes from wandering, exploring, and slowly uncovering.

Perception and the Mind's Camera

Just as a camera lens can be smudged or fogged, our perception can be distorted. We see the world not as it is, but as we perceive it to be. And often, what we see is shaped by old stories, past traumas, or unchallenged assumptions.

Imagine walking through life with a fingerprint on your camera lens. No matter what you try to capture, it'll be slightly off. That's what happens when we don't examine our own thoughts. We assume our perception is objective, but really, it's layered with bias and emotional residue.

We keep replaying adverse outcomes, failed relationships, disappointments—like a loop on a camera roll we forgot to delete. But just as we clean our phone screens and delete old files, we need to refresh our inner lens, too.

That process—of wiping the lens, adjusting the focus, finding new angles—is where transformation lives.

41

Joining the Dots

Life gives us moments. Dots. Random-feeling experiences that don't seem to add up—until one day, they do.

We all experience emotional dilemmas, moral crossroads, and mental roadblocks. At the time, they feel like distractions or failures. But in hindsight, they often form the exact constellation we needed.

There's a strange intelligence in how life unfolds. The delays, the confusion, the unexpected shifts—they all leave clues. And when we look back, we begin to connect those scattered dots into a picture we never planned, but always needed.

Dilemmas are not signs of failure. They're pressure points where growth is trying to break through. Avoiding them only leads to a looping pattern. But facing them—honestly, gently—lets us unravel the knots and restore clarity.

The Quiet Power of Not Knowing

There's a version of you that isn't obsessed with getting it right.

That version of you is calm in uncertainty. Open to possibility. Grounded in presence rather than perfection. That version of you is still here—beneath all the performance, the pressure, and the pretending.

The moment you realize that life doesn't need to be figured out all at once, you free yourself from the myth of control. You start seeing the blurry photos as beautiful. The unscripted conversations are sacred. The detours are divine.

Because when you stop rushing through the unknown, you begin to feel the truth of your own rhythm.

Final Invitation: Choose Presence Over Performance

If you've read this far, it means something in you is ready to step off the stage. To stop performing and start participating. It means you're tired of pretending you know exactly what you're doing—and ready to live with open hands.

You are not here to be perfect.

You are not here to impress anyone.

You are here to be whole.

And that wholeness won't come from filters, fixes, or five-year plans. It will come from quiet courage. From choosing presence over productivity. From learning to breathe when you don't know what's next.

Uncertainty isn't a problem to solve—it's a space to grow in. You can't control every outcome. But you can choose to stay present. To listen. To trust.

Because your soul has never needed certainty. It has only ever needed you.

42

Befriending Me - The Journey Back to Ourselves

43

Chapter 10

There comes a point in life—quietly, gradually, or all at once—when you realize that the most important relationship you will ever have... is the one you have with yourself.

Not romantic. Not familial. Not social.

Just you.

You, as you've been. You, as you are. You, as you're becoming.

But for most of us, this relationship has been quietly neglected, if not outright abandoned. We've been so busy reaching outward—searching for mirrors, for belonging, for proof of our worth—that we've overlooked the one person who's been there through it all.

Us.

The Loneliest Kind of Loneliness

We scroll endlessly. We share selectively. We search for connection in faces, texts, rooms, and posts. And yet, deep inside, something aches.

We think we're lonely because no one truly sees us.

But the deeper truth? We're lonely because we don't see ourselves.

Not really.

We become strangers to our own inner life. We perform roles. We give, support, inspire, and uplift. But quietly, in the silence between activities, we feel distant... from our own soul.

And the most painful part? We've been with ourselves the whole time.

The Mirror Moment

I remember one evening—simple, forgettable, except for one detail. I was walking past the hallway mirror, glass of wine in hand, background noise buzzing low. I'd had a normal day. Productive. "Fine." The kind of day that doesn't ask questions.

But the mirror caught me. Stopped me.

I looked into my own eyes, and they didn't look back like they knew me.

They looked tired. Not just physically. Spiritually. Like I had been ghosting my own presence for years. And it hit me, not in a dramatic, life-altering flash, but in a slow, bone-deep truth: I don't actually know myself anymore. I've been keeping myself company without ever offering myself companionship.

Why We Avoid Ourselves

We avoid ourselves in subtle ways: jokes that dismiss pain, routines that keep us busy, stories we tell to mask discomfort. We become skilled at justifying distance:

"I'm just tired."

"I'll deal with it later."

"That's not a big deal."

"I'm just overthinking."

But these aren't explanations. They're escapes.

Because facing ourselves means facing what hurts, what's broken, and what's been buried under our coping mechanisms.

And that kind of honesty demands courage—the kind we're rarely taught to hold.

Yet when we avoid ourselves, we create a deeper wound. Emotional, spiritual, and moral injury happens—not from being flawed, but from abandoning our own truth, from looking away when something inside us is asking to be seen.

The Dream of Someone Else

We grow up believing the ultimate comfort is someone else. Someone who gets us. Someone who listens and sees the real us. We dream of romantic partners, soul friends, the "one" who will sit with us in our rawest moments and still say, "You're safe with me."

But here's the truth: that someone must also be us.

Not instead of others. But before them.

Because even in the most intimate relationships, if we haven't befriended ourselves, we'll keep abandoning ourselves to be accepted. We'll keep seeking proof of worth instead of embodying it.

A Small Scene of Becoming

Maya, a freelance designer, once shared something with me. She went on a solo trip to Italy—imagining sunsets, soul-searching, and inspiration. But by day three, she found herself on a bench in Rome, eating a dry sandwich, overwhelmed with loneliness—not because she was alone, but because she didn't know how to be with herself.

No screen. No audience. No witness. Just her. And it terrified her.

Because being alone with yourself—without distractions—forces you to meet every layer you've avoided.

But it's also where true healing begins.

Real Friendship Starts in the Mundane

We often think self-love has to be loud: therapy, retreats, declarations. But befriending yourself is quieter. Softer.

It looks like:

Choosing strawberries at the store just for you, not because someone's coming over.

Speaking kindly to yourself when you mess up, instead of defaulting to shame.

Breathing deeply before reacting to a trigger—and gently asking, "What's this really about?"

Letting yourself rest without guilt.

Not laughing off something that hurt, just because you don't want to seem "dramatic."

It's in these small moments—how you speak to yourself in the silence—that the deepest bond is built.

44

When Emotions Come Late

Not every emotion announces itself when it's "appropriate."

When my father passed away, I didn't cry at the funeral. I shook hands, thanked people, and coordinated logistics. Everyone said I was "strong."

But I wasn't.

Weeks later, at a post office—of all places—I heard a child giggle. And something shattered. I sobbed in public, not knowing why the laugh cracked me open.

That's the thing about being a friend to yourself: it means not rushing your emotions. It means not performing neatness. It means trusting that your body knows when you're ready.

And when that moment comes, be there for you.

Understanding the Echoes

If we don't befriend ourselves, we misread our inner world. We mistake wounds for personality. We label fear as laziness. We call trauma "overreacting." We bury shame under humour. We distract instead of dissect.

But to truly know ourselves, we must stop making excuses for the places we avoid.

We must ask:

What keeps me from being still with myself?

Why do I run from the quiet?

What patterns am I repeating, and why?

What fear am I protecting, and what would happen if I faced it?

This is not self-judgment. This is a sacred excavation.

Because when we gently explore these questions, we start hearing the echoes of our own soul, longing to be heard.

Returning to the Truth

To befriend yourself means to stop lying to yourself.

It means honoring the parts of you that feel inconvenient or unlovable. It means tracing your triggers to their roots, not just trimming the branches. It means holding space for your own contradictions.

And when you do… something shifts.

You surrender.

Not in defeat, but in truth.

You begin surrendering to the realness of life. To the reality of your patterns. To the laws of nature and healing. To the divinity of being exactly as you are.

That surrender allows you to see your inner self, not just the version you hope others will approve of, but the raw, cracked, real you.

And you realize: this self, too, is worthy.

45

Voice Memo

I once started recording voice memos when I felt overwhelmed. Not to publish. Not to share. Just to hear myself. I would whisper:

"Hey, I know you're scared. It's okay. I'm with you."

Listening to those memos later broke me open in ways no one else ever could—because they were from me. A part of me I had long ignored finally reached out.

It made me wonder: How many years did I spend waiting for someone else to say the things I could say to myself?

The Shame We Don't Talk About

Almost everyone I've met carries a secret shame.

It sounds like:

"I'm too much."

"I ruin things."

"I'm a burden."

"If people really knew me, they'd leave."

These beliefs lodge themselves into our subconscious and begin shaping our lives. Not because they're true, but because they go unchallenged.

But the moment you begin treating yourself like a friend—not a problem—you start healing these core beliefs.

You replace shame with curiosity.

You replace judgment with understanding.

You stop abandoning yourself to feel accepted.

The Friend You've Been Looking For

If you take nothing else from this chapter, take this:

You don't need to become someone else to deserve love.

You don't need to earn your right to rest, softness, nourishment, or gentleness.

The friend you've been searching for—the one who understands without asking, who stays without needing, who listens without fixing—they are already inside you.

They've just been waiting for your return.

And when you finally say, "Hi... I've missed you,"—the healing begins.

46

Repository Beliefs

47

Chapter 11

Throughout our lives, we accumulate beliefs about ourselves, about others, and about the world around us. These beliefs often shape our actions and influence the way we perceive our circumstances. But what happens when those beliefs are no longer serving us? How do we let go of beliefs that no longer fit our evolving truth?

In this chapter, I explore the concept of repository beliefs—the belief systems we have stored within us, some of which we have outgrown. It's about recognizing when our old beliefs no longer serve us and learning to replace them with new, empowering truths.

There is a silent archive within us—a storage room of beliefs we didn't consciously choose, yet live by. These beliefs are inherited, absorbed, or self-generated from experiences shaped by fear, validation-seeking, and internalized conformity. These are the quiet, persistent thoughts that drive our behaviour without us realizing it. I call them repository beliefs—ideas and judgments embedded so deeply that we often mistake them for our own.

48

The Architecture of Internalized Belief

From a young age, we begin to gather impressions of the world and of ourselves, storing them in our subconscious. These impressions become silent convictions: I must be successful to be loved, Vulnerability is weakness, I need approval to feel worthy. These aren't always beliefs we examined or agreed with; many were formed out of necessity—to belong, to be safe, to be praised, to avoid pain.

These are our inner repository beliefs: quietly dictating our behaviour, influencing our identity, shaping how we interpret the world. The most dangerous part? We live by them without realizing they aren't our truth. They are echoes of our families, societies, traumas, and misunderstood moments.

We mistake inherited beliefs for intrinsic truths.

The Illusion of Conformity

Often, we find ourselves chasing versions of success, love, and self-worth that don't feel authentic—yet we chase them anyway. Why? Because we are unconsciously seeking validation. Validation not just from others, but from the internal judges we've created from others' expectations.

The mind, trained by years of exposure to these standards, feels a sense of failure when we don't meet them, even if they were never aligned with our truth. For instance, someone might feel like a disappointment for choosing peace over ambition, or experience guilt for not fitting into conventional gender roles. This isn't failure; it's dissonance between the true self and the internalized blueprint of who we were told to be.

Living under the weight of repository beliefs is exhausting. You begin to feel not just judged, but unknown. First by others, then eventually, by yourself.

Psychological Perspectives

Two major psychological theories give structure to these ideas:

Albert Bandura's Social Learning Theory

Bandura explains how people learn behaviours and internalize values through observation and imitation. As children, we pick up not just actions, but the emotional currency of those actions—how some behaviours are rewarded and others punished. Repository beliefs often form this way: by witnessing what brings acceptance and what invites rejection.

Cognitive Dissonance Theory (Leon Festinger)

This theory describes the inner conflict we feel when we hold two contradictory beliefs, or when our behaviours contradict our values. Repository beliefs cause such dissonance when they no longer fit our truth, but rather than challenge them, we suppress ourselves. This leads to guilt, self-criticism, and a deepening sense of inauthenticity.

49

The Danger of Deepening Distance

The longer we live by beliefs that don't resonate with us, the more disconnected we become from who we truly are. Over time, the distance between our authentic self and our conditioned identity widens. This disconnect can grow so deep that we forget what our own voice sounds like. We become strangers to ourselves.

What's terrifying is how easily these beliefs can be passed on. Not because we want to, but because we haven't questioned them. We might tell our children the same stories we were told: about what success means, about what emotions are acceptable, about who they should become to be loved. Without reflection, the cycle continues—generation after generation.

It's not just dangerous. It's destructive. These beliefs become internal barriers that block us from growth. They make us resistant to change because they anchor us to a version of ourselves that no longer exists. And yet, letting go feels like a betrayal of family, tradition, or even identity. That's the trap.

Eventually, the disconnect grows so wide that we risk losing our connection to our root self altogether. We start confusing our programming with our personality. We stop questioning. We stop growing.

50

Challenging the Internal Archive

So, how do we move forward?

We challenge the archive. Not with force, but with curiosity. We ask:

Where did this belief come from?

Who benefits from my believing this?

What would my life look like without this belief?

Some beliefs will stay. They'll evolve with you. Others will fall away the moment you realize they were never yours. You must be willing to step outside of your own perception and see the world from a new lens—a lens that is uniquely yours, shaped by your intuition, your lived experiences, your evolving self.

This shift won't just change your inner world. It will ripple outward, creating space for others to live more freely, too. That's how societal transformation begins—one person questioning, one belief at a time.

Excavating the Archive

There was a time I confused adaptation with identity. I tried to become who I thought I needed to be in order to belong, achieve, and be worthy. But every performance pulled me further from my own voice. I've come to see that the thoughts I once clung to—the warnings, the rules, the beliefs about what I could or could not do—were never mine to begin with. They were hand-me-downs, offered with good intentions, but heavy with unseen costs. Releasing them hasn't been easy. It has required courage to sit with discomfort, to feel unmoored, to challenge not just the world's version of me, but my own internalized one. Yet in that unravelling, I've found glimpses of clarity—of who I am beneath the roles, beneath the rules. That clarity doesn't come all at once; it arrives in fragments, quiet moments of resonance, a sense of returning. The more I release what doesn't belong to me, the more space I create for something real, something rooted. My journey is not about finding a new identity—it's about coming home to the one that was always there, waiting beneath the noise.

51

Real-Life Echoes

52

Chapter 12
Listening to the Voices Within Others

We are not alone in our inner battles. Though our echoes may sound different—louder for some, softer for others—they all come from the same place: the intersection of survival, emotion, memory, and meaning.

As this book closes, I wanted to end not with theory or abstraction, but with humanity. With truth. With the voices of real people who, like all of us, have been living through their own echoes—facing, questioning, falling, adapting, grieving, and becoming.

I interviewed five individuals—each anonymous, each unique, each unfiltered. I didn't ask them for solutions. I asked for their realities. Their raw truths. Their philosophies and paradoxes. What you'll read here is not polished. It is not inspirational in a traditional sense. It is deeper than that. It is real.

And in their stories, you may find pieces of your own.

53

Introduction to the Interviews
For this reflective study, I asked a series of inward-facing questions—not for factual answers, but for emotional truths. These were questions meant to stir echoes rather than provide conclusions:

What does it mean to adapt?

What is a "moment" to you?

What is the apparent truth, and how does it relate to profit, loss, and identity?

What does it mean to "die" emotionally or spiritually in this life?

Do value and respect mean the same thing? Which comes first for you?

How do you experience thoughts and feelings, and which are most present now?

What is the weight and balance of your inner dialogue?

How do you define rest, productivity, racing, and slowing down?

And perhaps most intimately: Who are you, in your own eyes?

These aren't just questions. They are emotional excavations. Invitations to dig beneath the surface and face ourselves, as we are.

54

Echo 1: The Observer and the Rebuilder

Echo 1 offered reflections that were both analytical and poetic. There's a rhythm to how they process life—a way of observing pain without dramatizing it, and of adapting without abandoning the core self.

Adaptation and Moments

"Adaptation happens on an everyday basis," Echo 1 shares with quiet conviction. "When your comfort zone begins to feel uncomfortable, that's when real adaptation starts."

They don't describe adaptation as something you prepare for in advance. Instead, it arrives quietly, often in discomfort. "I've learned that it's better to adapt now than to suffer later."

When asked what counts as a "moment," Echo 1's definition is intimate: "A moment is anything that significantly alters how I perceive the world, how I see myself. It changes my vision, my individuality, and my attitude toward life. A moment isn't about time—it's about shift."

Apparent Truth, Profit, and Identity

Truth is a deeply personal subject for Echo 1. "I've often tricked myself into accepting my version of the truth as the absolute reality," they admit. "Apparent truth feels more manageable—it's in my control."

But there's a deeper tension beneath that. "If you use truth to measure gain or loss, then it's no longer truth—it's a manipulation. The real truth stands apart from those calculations. You either choose truth, or you choose to live within the economy of profit and loss. They don't coexist."

Their most significant insight? "My biggest gain in life has been learning to be truthful with myself. That kind of integrity doesn't seek approval or benefit—it seeks alignment."

Dying Before Dying

"I believe we should die a little every day," Echo 1 says, not in despair but with sincerity. "But unfortunately, it doesn't happen like that."

Their emotional deaths didn't occur during catastrophes, but in silence. "The times I truly 'died' inside were the moments I tried my hardest to survive alone. That's when I realized—self-preservation without connection isn't survival. It's isolation."

Value vs. Respect

"There's a difference between value and respect," they say. "For me, value comes first. I value humanity above status. But in a world that rewards appearances, that choice comes with pain."

Echo 1 divides people into two groups: "Those who chase status out of fear, and those who seek it from a desire to grow. Both exist. But I've always chosen value first."

Their measure of character isn't reputation—it's memory. "People won't remember your credentials. But they'll remember how you treated them."

55

On Emotions and Thought Patterns

"No feeling comes alone," Echo 1 reflects. "There's always a thought before it. Feelings don't just appear—they are triggered."

They don't shy away from feelings. In fact, they approach them like a skill to be cultivated. "It's like learning to drive a car. At first, you're scared. But once you get comfortable with the emotions, you gain control. The more I allow myself to feel, the more grounded I become."

Echo 1 believes that emotions can be witnessed without being overwhelmed by them. "People often avoid their emotions because they're afraid of losing control. But to me, embracing emotion is part of building a healthy relationship with myself."

The Balance and Weight of Thoughts

"There's no such thing as a perfect balance of thoughts," Echo 1 says. "Thoughts come with their own intensity. Some are heavy, some light."

Rather than trying to balance them equally, they focus on giving the right thoughts the right amount of space. "When I manage that well, I don't suffer. When I can't, I do."

For them, balance isn't equilibrium—it's discernment. "It's not about silencing thoughts. It's about learning which ones deserve volume, and which ones don't."

56

Rest, Rhythm, and Self-Pacing

Their thoughts on rest and productivity reflect a grounded philosophy:

Sleep is essential. "It's how I learn to rise again and feel proud of having made it through another day."

Rest is a pause, not a complete stop. "We need to rest, but not quit."

Awake is the clarity that makes you appreciate rest.

Productivity is self-defined. "I decide what it means for me, and I add rest to make it sustainable."

Racing is energizing—but only until you hit exhaustion. "It reminds me of my limits."

Slowing down isn't scheduled—it happens when the pace becomes unsustainable. "I try to move at a pace that doesn't burn me out."

Who Are You?

When asked this most vulnerable question, Echo 1 takes a long pause. And then they say:

"I'm a friend to myself first. A learner. Emotionally sensitive. Sometimes chaotic, but trying. I'm both the best gift I've received and the greatest work in progress I know.

I am the blueprint of my own becoming. My own hero and my own critic. A warrior who sometimes falls apart, but never gives up on rebuilding.

The worst version of me? The one who disconnects and manipulates to survive.

The best? The one trying—genuinely—to understand who I truly am beneath all the layers."

Why These Echoes Matter

Echo 1's voice may feel uniquely theirs, but in it, many of us will hear our own reflections. The doubts. The recalibrations. The longing to be seen by oneself. The effort to balance inner chaos with quiet wisdom.

This chapter isn't about offering answers—it's about holding space. Each story is a permission slip to feel more deeply, to reflect more honestly, and to trust that within our most unpolished truths lie our most human moments.

And this is just one voice.

57

Echo 2: The Mindset Leaper

Echo 2's journey is defined by a profound transformation—a leap from the security of a job into the uncertainty of entrepreneurship. It is a story of courage, reinvention, and the constant dance between logic and instinct.

Adaptation Through Total Mindset Shift

"Moving from a stable job to starting my own business was terrifying," Echo 2 confesses. "But I thought of myself as a hero who needed to take that leap."

Adaptation, they explain, wasn't born of necessity—it came from reframing everything, from their sense of identity, family roles, friendships, and spirituality. "When I shifted everything—my worldview, relationships, even what I believed in—that's when I began to truly adapt."

This kind of transformation wasn't incremental—it was immersive. They embraced change not just in action, but at the level of being.

On Moments, Truth, Profit, and Loss

Echo 2 does not believe in one fixed truth. "Apparent truth," they say, "is a perception. Seeing and perceiving are different. Truth is bound to change." This is not resignation—it is liberation.

They understand that profit or loss in life is a shifting equation. One day's success can become another day's regret. "I've experienced that twice—emotional disasters that made the world feel like it ended."

They admit to once being a skilled manipulator—not maliciously, but strategically. Now, they are more direct. "If you live from your heart, peace becomes the real profit. Lies may bring short-term gain, but long-term emptiness."

That difference—truth versus profit—is a pivotal theme in their story.

Moments of Dying and Rebirth

Echo 2 has "died" several times—not in physical terms, but emotionally. "There were moments I felt utterly worthless. I broke someone's trust, and for me, that was the end of my self-worth."

In those moments, they lost their sense of existence. "It was a total collapse." But each of these "deaths" revealed a self-realization—sometimes painful, sometimes freeing, always essential.

Value, Respect, and Relationships

For Echo 2, respect still holds weight, but not above personal integrity. They choose value over respect. "Respect means little if it costs your soul," they reflect.

In relationships, this becomes intimate: "Friends and enemies alike showed me what truly serves me." They speak of living through loneliness and discovering deeper, more intimate moments after being alone for too long.

Thoughts, Feelings, Balance

Thoughts, to them, are cumbersome, laden with weight and repetition. They balance them deliberately. "When my mind races, like in business, it burdens me. But when I slow down, I become mindful."

They describe the emotional escapism many know: "I used to run from difficult emotions. But the moment I accepted them, peace came."

To them, feelings aren't inconvenient—they're essential markers that guide self-care and growth.

Rhythm of Existence

Sleep = healing medicine
Rest = nightly relaxation
Awake = dawned awareness
Productivity = meaningful action

Racing = life's inevitable fast moments

Slowing Down = mindful living, even if it sometimes brings discomfort or physical tension

58

Facing Identity

Echo 2 identifies as a blend of roles:

"I am a father. I am a friend. I am a teacher and a consultant. I see myself as calm, responsible, and confident, although I also feel overwhelmed at times."

They are honest about Vulnerability: "Sometimes, I wish I could let everything go. Other times, solitude brings joy. My worst moments are when I cannot understand people or when I've trusted wrongly."

Emerging Presence

When describing their inner world, Echo 2 says:

"Thoughts can be enemies—if time isn't on your side. Sometimes I feel defeated, but I still want to love myself."

This tender acknowledgment—wanting self-love even amidst inner conflict—reveals a person engaged in honest companionship with themselves.

Echo 2 in a Snapshot

Echo 2's story is one of transformation:

A bold step into uncertainty.

A mindset rebuilt from the ground up.

A learning that truth and profit cannot coexist.

A witnessing of personal death and emotional rebirth.

A life lived responsibly, vulnerably, and with mindful intention.

In Echo 2, we find many fragments:

The bravery to leap.

The cost of reinvention.

The reality of contradictory feelings.

The weight and relief of accepting ourselves.

And perhaps, a reflection of what each of us faces when we quietly ask ourselves:

Am I being true to who I am, beyond validation, beyond fear?

59

Echo 3: The One Who Broke and Chose to Heal

Echo 3's journey begins not with action but with isolation—a long-standing adaptation to loneliness, both physical and emotional. They are not someone who merely survived hard times but someone who chose to reflect deeply on what those moments meant and how they changed them.

Adapting to Loneliness, Then Learning to Cherish

"I adapted by being alone," Echo 3 shares. "I had to." Their life, at certain points, felt marked by solitude—but in that silence, clarity emerged.

Over time, they began to collect and treasure what they called "cherishable moments"—little pieces of life, small or big, that grounded them. It's not the size of the moment, but its meaning that matters.

The Fluidity of Truth

For Echo 3, the truth is not fixed. "There is no 'apparent truth,'" they say. "Nothing is forever. Truth can be painful or freeing—but it changes."

They face a hard dilemma: "If I say the truth, I lose things. If I lie, I may gain something briefly. But in the long run, only truth gives peace." This internal negotiation between honesty and consequence has been central to their emotional journey.

60

Emotional Deaths and Self-Forgiveness

"I've felt unworthy—three specific times in my life," Echo 3 recalls. "Once, I broke someone's trust, and in that moment, I felt I had no right to exist."

These were not dramatic external events, but quiet, internal collapses—the kind that redefine a person from within. Yet, from these collapses came reflection, then the beginning of self-compassion.

They now understand that these difficult feelings don't need to be escaped, but accepted. "I used to run. Now, when I accept my emotions, I feel blissful. I feel real."

Value and Respect: Deeply Entwined

For Echo 3, value and respect are intertwined. "They feel like the same thing to me," they say. "But both can be painful when missing."

They don't isolate feelings or label them as good or bad—rather, they observe them, like weather patterns passing through. "Negative feelings, I try to escape. But once I accept them, I feel peace."

61

The Weight and Balance of Thoughts
Thoughts are often heavy for Echo 3, sometimes without a clear reason. "Even when things seem okay, my thoughts weigh me down." Yet, despite that heaviness, they strive for emotional balance.

"I've realized that the weight of thought doesn't always mean something's wrong. It just means I'm deeply engaged with what's happening."

The Language of Energy
Sleep = medicine
Rest = the comfort of night
Awake = the beauty of dawn
Productivity = action, moving forward
Racing = the flow of life
Slowing down = physical pain, but also reflection

These words aren't just metaphors to Echo 3—they are states of being. Each word contains memory, feeling, and experience.

62

Seeing the Self: Strength and Solitude

"I am a mother," they say. "A teacher. A confident human being who faces problems with calmness and determination." Yet beneath that identity lies Vulnerability: "Sometimes I feel deeply lonely, even in company. Sometimes I just want to let go of everything."

Still, solitude, when chosen, becomes sacred. "'There are times when being alone feels like joy."

Their worst feeling is not loss, but not understanding people. "I trusted the wrong people. That hurts more than anything." And yet, through pain, there's a clear voice: "Even after the worst, the faith from within... It's still there."

Relationship with Thoughts

Echo 3 describes a love-hate relationship with their inner world. "Sometimes, thoughts are enemies. Other times, they help. It depends on time, place, and mood."

They admit they can't fully control their mind, but that doesn't stop them from trying to love them. "I want to love myself. I have that tendency."

63

Echo 3 in a Snapshot
Echo 3 lives in a world of nuance:
They've suffered emotional deaths and still rise.
They question every truth but live by honesty.
They feel deeply—but are not ruled by feelings.
They've chosen to accept rather than escape.
Their strength is quiet, rooted not in bold action but in deep reflection.

64

Echo 4: The One Who Walked Alone Through Grief

Echo 4's life shifted permanently after a deep personal loss. Grief arrived unannounced and unwelcome, and it demanded not just mourning, but transformation. This Echo doesn't speak of overcoming grief, but of learning to walk with it.

Grief as Catalyst for Inner Balance

After the demise of a loved one, Echo 4 found themselves unable to accept reality. "I was lost. Expectations broke. I couldn't look at life the same way anymore." They began navigating life independently, not by choice but by necessity, balancing responsibilities and emotions in silence.

"I tried to manage everything by myself," they reflect. "And in doing so, I discovered the strength I didn't know I had."

Redefining Moments and Truth

For Echo 4, "joyful moments" are what they now look forward to—not grand achievements, but small windows of light. "When I feel joy, that's the moment I look up to. That's when I know I'm still here."

Truth, in their view, is relational. "There's no such thing as an absolute truth," they say. "You speak your truth depending on the situation and who you're speaking to."

This doesn't mean they live without integrity. It means they recognize that truth is not static—it lives in context, and must sometimes bend for kindness, understanding, or survival.

On Profit, Loss, and Living Fully

"I've never seen life in terms of profit and loss," Echo 4 states clearly. "Every moment, I've died a little. And every moment, I've lived a little too."

Their life isn't measured in gain or success, but in presence, in simply continuing.

Respect First, Then Value

"Respect comes before values for me," they say. "When someone disrespects me, it hits deep—it brings regret and heaviness."

They share an experience of being recently "disvalued," a moment that reminded them of how tightly respect is woven into their sense of emotional safety.

When Thoughts Hurt, But Are Still Accepted

"When my thoughts become heavy, it hurts," Echo 4 confesses. "But I've learned to accept them."

This acceptance is not resignation—it is a quiet resilience. The ability to sit with discomfort without running from it.

65

The Inner Dictionary: Defining Life's States

Sleeping = a good feeling, a reset

Awake = joy, presence

Resting = relaxation, a gentle pause

Productivity = working, living a balanced life

Racing = the pace of life

Slowing down = a conscious decision to live fully, not just function

These aren't just states of energy for Echo 4—they are reflections of a rhythm they now choose to honour.

Who They Are: Self-Sculpted

Echo 4's sense of identity is not loud, but clear. "My life is structured by my own hands," they say. In this structure, they find dignity and peace.

Their greatest feeling is honesty—a deep alignment with their inner truth. The worst feeling is betrayal—" being deceived by someone I trusted."

Yet, they continue to trust, to try, to live fully.

Echo 4 in a Snapshot

Echo 4 has walked through grief without a guide.

They trust moments of joy and honesty as signs they're still healing.

They define truth through compassion and respect as a form of emotional currency.

They accept pain as a companion—but not as a master.

Their strength is quite endurance. Their life is a mosaic of resilience.

Echo 5: The One Learning to Let Go

Echo 5 is someone who has chosen acceptance, not passivity, but the active, courageous work of surrender. They have made peace with what cannot be controlled and are learning to meet life on its own terms.

Adapting to Time and Change

For Echo 5, the most difficult adaptation wasn't external—it was internal. "The hardest thing," they say, "was adapting to time—to change—and accepting that I can't always hold on."

They speak of learning how to stay mentally joyful, of not breaking down too often, and of practicing forgiveness, both of others and of themselves.

"It's about letting go of the past. Forgiving more. And moving through life with ease, not force."

On Fleeting Moments and the Challenge of Presence

Moments, for Echo 5, are elusive. "Moments come and go. Trying to hold onto them is almost impossible."

They admit that nostalgia often pulls them backward, especially when memories of the past resurface. Yet, this nostalgia doesn't paralyse them. It only deepens their desire to stay present: "Trying to stop a moment is very tough. But I try."

66

Love as Apparent Truth

When asked about apparent truth, Echo 5 answers simply: "Apparent truth is love." It's not something abstract or philosophical—it's felt.

"Living a life full of lies makes you want to escape. It weakens you. Truth, even when hard, brings peace. Lies complicate things."

They are honest about the contradiction: truth is hard, but lies are harder. Love, even when painful, still feels like truth.

On Profit, Loss, and Breaking Down

To Echo 5, profit and loss are not just material—they are emotional currencies.

"There's some profit in life, and some loss too. I've felt dead many times—not physically, but emotionally. Losing someone, or not understanding them when they were alive, felt like a death in me."

But these moments also became teachers.

"Now I'm learning step by step. Trying to make life normal again. Trying to understand it better."

Respect and the Complexity of Self-Understanding

The line between respect and loss is razor-thin for Echo 5.

"The worst time was not understanding someone when I had the chance. I wish I had spent more time with the people I loved."

They now understand that respect is not just shown to others—it's something we owe ourselves, especially in grief, in regret, in healing.

Manipulation, Forgiveness, and the Importance of Relationships

Echo 5 acknowledges past manipulation—not malicious, but self-protective. They now see friendship as sacred.

"Manipulation once felt like survival. Now, I know friendship is more important. Relationships are where life happens."

They are not proud of everything in the past. But they are not ashamed either. They are becoming.

Defining States of Being

Sleeping = recovery

Resting = medicine for the soul

Awake = presence

Productivity = doing something meaningful, not just being busy

Racing = a reflection of urgency

Slowing down = understanding the body and mind, embracing calm

Each word carries emotional weight—these are not routines, but reflections of an inner world in motion.

67

Who They Are Becoming

Echo 5 defines themself not by labels, but by intentions:

"I'm trying to be more myself. I wish to know how to break more—to be softer, more real."

They are slowly dismantling the parts of themselves that hardened over time. Not to fall apart—but to fall into place.

Echo 5 in a Snapshot

Echo 5 is learning to let go—not out of weakness, but out of strength.

They carry the ache of past regrets, but they choose love over guilt.

They define truth by the simplicity of being real, not right.

Their journey is not about perfection, but peaceful progress.

They are not just surviving life. They are starting to live it.

68

We Are All Echoes

Each of these voices—each Echo—offered a glimpse into a profoundly personal terrain. And yet, as different as their answers were, they all traced a similar path: from survival to awareness, from fear to courage, from confusion to clarity, from self-doubt to self-definition.

Some battled isolation.
Some grieved the loss.
Some questioned the truth.
Some chose love.
All of them faced themselves.

What these Echoes remind us is that life is never lived in a straight line. It bends. It collapses. It begins again. They show us that even the most ordinary life contains extraordinary depth—if we are willing to listen.

They've made peace with contradictions: that strength can appear as softness, that breaking down is sometimes the first step toward healing, that respect and value don't always arrive together, and that truth is not fixed—it breathes with us.

They've told us:

That adapting doesn't mean losing yourself—it means meeting who you are now.

Those moments, however fleeting, are where life happens.

That inner chaos is not failure—it's a necessary storm.

Those feelings can be teachers. Thoughts can be heavy, but they are not immovable.

That rest is not weakness. Slowing down is not failure. And racing is not the only pace that matters.

Above all, they've reminded us of something simple and profound: We are not alone.

We are all Echoes—shaped by time, love, loss, choices, and hope.

We speak differently, but we seek the same: truth, connection, and peace within ourselves.

So, as you finish this book, maybe ask yourself:

What are the echoes within you trying to say?

And when was the last time you truly listened?

Let that be your next beginning.

69

The Journey Continues

70

The journey doesn't end when the last word is read or the last page is turned. It doesn't end when the lights dim or the music fades. It continues—in silences, in shadows, in the smallest folds of thought that linger. This book may be closing, but your mind is still open, still echoing, still alive.

You've walked with me through memories, through questions, through truths that were perhaps once too quiet to hear. But now—now they have a voice. Yours.

The fireworks began to bloom in the sky with passing time, and I—still, silent, aware—stood watching, not as a spectator, but as a soul becoming. In that burst of light, I felt it: I was no longer searching for meaning. I was the meaning. Obsessively, compulsively, I am in love with my soul—not for its perfection, but for its honest chaos. It's broken beauty. It's resilience.

Somewhere along this path, I started believing in moments that reflect eternity. The ones that don't need to be loud to be heard. The ones that feel like a whisper and hit like a wave. Time doesn't belong to us—it never did. But the tick-tock of the watch on my wrist reminds me: I can choose how I spend what time I have. And there is grace in that.

Who waits till the end of the show? Who decides how long it should go on? Or is it the waiting itself, the not knowing, that gives the show its meaning? We measure things—time, worth, success—but rarely do we measure depth. And when I ask myself these things today, it matters. It finally matters.

This journey was never just mine. Memories, thoughts, conversations, and quiet realizations—they've all been characters in this unfolding play. Some stayed behind the wings, never seen, but deeply felt. Some whispered lines from behind the curtains, shaping the story in ways I may never fully understand. And then, there were those who stood beside me, scene after scene, reminding me: I was never truly alone.

The characters matter. The script may be incomplete. But the presence, the intention—that's where the soul of the story lives.

And yes—the echoes matter. They are not just leftover noise; they are messages. Warnings. Invitations. They are fragments of who we were, and glimpses of who we are becoming. Every Echo is a reminder that something once lived—and that something still does.

The audience? They're here too. Some come to see. Some to understand. Some just to criticize. But even that—is part of the story. Every reaction, every silence, every clap... it all builds to that final moment, where you find yourself standing with yourself, no longer afraid of the spotlight, no longer hiding in the wings.

And when the curtain falls?

There will be silence. The kind that feels sacred. The kind that doesn't end something but honours it.

That's where the journey truly continues—not on a stage, not in a book, but in the inner stillness where your truth quietly waits to be lived.

So go on. Ask more questions. Break more patterns. Fall in love with your soul, over and over again. Be messy. Be human. Be whole. This is not the end.

It never was.

The journey continues.
And the echoes live on.

71

The Echoes of the Mind

In a world that moves faster than we can feel, Echoes of the Mind invites you to pause.

This is not a book that tells you what to fix.

It's a space to remember what you already know.

A place for the identities you've shed, the thoughts you've silenced, the truths you carry quietly beneath the surface.

With poetic clarity and radical tenderness, Shiny —author of The Tunnel-offers a soft rebellion against the noise. Her words do not chase resolution.

They listen. They linger. They illuminate.

This book is for anyone who has ever looked in the mirror and whispered,

"Is this really me?"

She doesn't promise clarity.

She creates the space for it.

And sometimes, that's where healing begins.

Shiny never intended to become a writer.

Trained in microbiology and marine biology, her early life followed the quiet rhythms of science and the sea. But when everything she knew unraveled, writing came—not as ambition, but as survival.

What began in an old yellow notebook became a lifelong conversation with truth. She writes from silence, from the in-between, from the place where feeling begins before language forms, She has no writing rituals, only a page, a pen, and the willingness to be honest.

For more reflections, quiet truths, and unspoken thoughts: livingbeyondbarrier_o

www.ingramcontent.com/pod-product-compliance
Lightning Source LLC
Chambersburg PA
CBHW030603010526
44109CB00059B/1226